Parapet

To Chris-
felin

voyageur

from

Tom

17 . 3 . 14

TOM HUBBARD's previous poetry collections include:

Four Fife Poets (with John Brewster, William Hershaw
and the late Harvey Holton; Aberdeen
University Press)
Isolde's Luve-Daith (Akros)
Tak 5/Tak 50 (CD; with William Hershaw, Angus Martin,
David C. Purdie and David Purves;
Scotsoun)
Scottish Faust: Poems and Ballads of Eldritch Lore (Kettillonia)
From Soda Fountain to Moonshine Mountain: American Poems
(Akros)
Peacocks and Squirrels: Poems of Fife (Akros)
The Chagall Winnocks: wi ither Scots Ballants and Poems o
Europe (Book with CD; Grace Note
Publications)
The Nyaff (Windfall Books)
The Merry Dancers (with Sheena Blackhall; Malfranteaux
Concepts)

His novel, *Marie B.* (Ravenscraig Press), is based on the life
of the Ukrainian painter Marie Bashkirtseff

His non-fictional books include:

Seeking Mr Hyde: Studies in Robert Louis Stevenson,
Symbolism, and the Pre-Modern (Peter Lang)
The Integrative Vision: Poetry and the Visual Arts in Baudelaire,
Rilke, and MacDiarmid (Akros)
Michael Scot: Myth and Polymath (Akros)

Parapets and Labyrinths
Poems in English and Scots
on European themes 1984-2012

Tom Hubbard

Je regrette l'Europe et ses anciens parapets.
RIMBAUD

Grace Note
Publications

PARAPETS AND LABYRINTHS first published, 2013
by GRACE NOTE PUBLICATIONS C.I.C.

GRACE NOTE PUBLICATIONS
Grange of Locherlour,
Ochtertyre, PH7 4JS,
Scotland

books@gracenotereading.co.uk
www.gracenotepublications.co.uk

ISBN 978-1-907676-23-9

Portrait of TOM HUBBARD by ALLAN MCMILLAN,
reproduced with permission

THE COVER DESIGN incorporates *Europa and
the Bull* by the Ukrainian artist
ARKADY PUGACHEVSKY.

Details of the original work:
ex libris Sergey Brodovich, colour engraving,
75x109mm, 2007.
The engraving is reproduced by kind permission of the artist

Please visit these websites:
http://brodovych.com/publications/2288/Arkady+Pugachevsky.html
http://pugachevsky.name

IN MEMORIAM GEORGE BRUCE 1909-2002

CONTENTS

PREFACE

A lithograph by the Dutch artist M.C. Escher, **Relativity,** displays an interior in which stairways go up and down, and back again, in a dizzying perspective, where depending on the observer of the lithograph, perspective continually shifts, in which 'up' can easily be perceived as 'down', or even sideways, and vice versa; we can also catch a glimpse of gardens, trees and a table laid out for lunch outside. It could be the interior of a monastery, or some madman's castle. Escher's art chimes in with the 'parapets and labyrinths' explored in Tom Hubbard's poetry. The parapets are remnants of the feudal past, and after all the feudal system lasted much longer than the capitalist one has so far. The labyrinths suggested by the poems remind us of nothing less than the labyrinth of European history, its traumas and upheavals, especially in the twentieth century, but now seen from an emerging 21st century perspective.

A good number of European countries came within the poet's purview. He resided in or visited them in his various posts as guest lecturer in Scottish Literature, and also inter-disciplinary cultural studies. But the poet wears his learning lightly, more of a cultivated 'flâneur' than a stuffy academic. Spain is one of the countries which figures in these poems, with a cameo

1

of Toledo, as painted by El Greco, the cityscape electrically charged by thunder and lightning. The poem is prefaced by comments on Michael Scot, 'the Scottish polymath who had based himself in Toledo', and was widely regarded as a wizard, one could say a 'Wizard of the North', long before Walter Scott. Michael Scot is in some ways the poet's alter-ego; just like the wizard he makes himself at home everywhere.

Some of the poems are what the poet calls 'transcreations', others are his own, some are in Scots, and others in English, but all are touched with the imaginative power of a poet adept at formulating an 'integrative vision', a term that the poet himself applied to Baudelaire in his book of that title. One of the finest poems here, 'Berlioz at Meylan', brings that flamboyant composer and his haunts to turbulent life; another, 'Speirins', endows demotic energy to perhaps Brecht's best-loved poem, one which nevertheless sounds too prosy and even slight when rendered into standard English translation. 'Candles', inspired by a trip to Poland in 1989 when the nation was beginning to shake off the shackles of Communism, is a very moving tribute to the resilience of the Poles. There are no less than four poems associated with Hungary, and indeed Hungary was Edwin Morgan's model of a nation struggling to be free, as he expressed it in 'Louis Kossuth', one of his late dramatic monologues. About two of the poems by a Hungarian translated here, the poet tells us that 'the resulting ironies … are not unfamiliar to the socially-existentialist conflicts of expat Scots'. With the first poem here, 'The Retour o Troilus', we are brought back to Fife, where the poet lives. It is a fine homage to the makar from Dunfermline, Robert Henryson. One of Scotland's greatest poets, he was second perhaps only to Burns, and the equal of Chaucer.

If there is anything labyrinthine about these poems, it is because the poet is no mere aficionado of the 'grand tour', but sharply observant, knowing there is nothing straightforward about Europe and its outlying archipelago of the British Isles, Ireland and Iceland. Geographically, it is a labyrinth which leads to Paris, or London, or Brussels, but whose centre is nowhere, so it also leads to the varied places, well-known or otherwise, in these poems. As the poet puts it in 'The Terrace at Basel', an agreeably Arnoldian piece:

> *Now couples amble by the parapet's*
> *Vista of history and its regrets; …*

But history be damned. Darkness may be latent in many of the poems, but as these lines suggest, the pleasure principle trumps everything else in the poetry of Tom Hubbard.

Mario Relich
Edinburgh, Jan. 2013

INTRODUCTION: SPACES

1

The sea, wrote Baudelaire, gives us at once the notion of immensity and movement; a mere six or seven leagues can suggest infinity – infinity in miniature, as it were.

I live on the east coast of Fife, and Baudelaire's words often come back to me. During the summer of 2011, at The Boathouse in Aberdour, my friend the sculptor Kenny Munro curated an exhibition of the work of George Wyllie, that unique figure in the visual arts of twentieth / twenty-first centuries Scotland. Here was immensity – and movement (even a still sculpture can suggest that!) – of a man's life-work, held within the space of a gallery right on the shore. At the show's opening, Richard Demarco pointed to the window facing the sea: the exhibition was in a sense continued by the breathtaking panorama beyond. In other words, the Boathouse both contained the works but didn't contain them: there was an outflow, so to speak, to the natural environment. I would see this as (1) a complex dynamic operating within the limited space of the Boathouse (a labyrinth), augmented by (2) the expansive space of the coastal view (a parapet).

The exhibition contained many examples of George's trademark boats and other maritime images, together with hilarious video footage of his clowning with the actor Bill Paterson. George's laughter was the mark of a man who was serious but never solemn; as Busoni put it, 'Humour is the blossom on the tree of profundity.' Some of the images accompanied poems, including one by Tessa Ransford. I had long known that George was deeply interested in arts other than his own – always the sign of a visionary – as he had visited the Scottish Poetry Library in the course of his searches. At the Aberdour show, there was one piece which took its cue from Rimbaud's 'Le bateau ivre' – 'The Drunken Boat' – and I found myself wishing that George Wyllie had known and met another independent spirit who had once worked further up the Fife coast. What a conversation they might have enjoyed, for the Anstruther man was the makar Alastair Mackie (1925-95) who had transcreated that same Rimbaud poem into Scots as 'The Drucken Boat'. The original poem provides the epigraph for the present book.

Alastair Mackie knew both the parapet of his viewpoint from his back-green, celebrated in his poetry, and the labyrinth of his personal demons (over which his art was no mean triumph). 'A herbour is a tension atween twa pulls,' he wrote, 'the beck o horizons and the rug o hame.' For me, these lines sum up much of what I took from the George Wyllie show. It's pleasant to record here that Alastair Mackie's collected poems appeared last year: those responsible for this splendid volume deserve Scotland's gratitude, and, more to the point, its attention.

It would be too simple, too pat, to regard parapets as liberating and labyrinths as constraining. Parapets can be defensive, and therefore tense, places: from the esplanade at Kirkcaldy I enjoy a great prospect but I

5

can also see the anti-tank barriers placed on the shore by exiled Polish soldiers. Labyrinths can be places of discovery: of things sinister, to be sure, but also of personal growth – think of the caves in Mark Twain's *Tom Sawyer*, of the threat there of Injun Joe with his bowie-knife, but also of young Tom and Becky on the cusp of adolescence, as they negotiate the passages by spluttering candlelight.

It was in the south of France, a year ago, that at last I was able to make a pilgrimage to a work of art which had long fascinated me. In its way, this piece is both parapet and labyrinth, and in that respect it's in a line from the great myths of Europa and the bull, Crete, Knossos, Ariadne and the Minotaur.

2

You can stumble and tumble upon it while you're engaged with everyday banalities. It's the incident, small in itself, which can lead to a triumph of creativity. It happened to a provincial French postman, Ferdinand Cheval, during one of his rounds: he lost his footing against a stone which he then picked up and admired for its strange shape. He decided to take it home to his yard. Cheval – or 'Facteur [postman] Cheval' as he's best known - continued to collect more stones as he went about his business, and resolved to make a reality of a long-nurtured fantasy. In that open space by his home at Hauterives, south of Lyon, he would construct his Palais Idéal – his ideal palace – working on it for as long as it would take.

It took him over thirty years, from 1879 to 1912. It's the oddest building you're ever likely to visit in a lifetime, let alone within thirty-odd years. For some it has been an eyesore, the creation of a village crank. For André Malraux, the French minister of culture in 1969, it deserved the status of a national monument, as the world's sole example of 'architecture naïve'. *Sole* example? What about follies, such as Jack the Treacle-Eater in Somerset, or Scotland's own outsized Pineapple at Airth near the Kincardine Bridges? When I lived in Leixlip, Ireland, I was within walking distance of Co. Kildare's ziggurat, the 'Wonderful Barn', and there was a Gothick lodge and a circular temple in the ample grounds of nearby Castletown House. Most of these weird structures owe their existence to aristocratic or otherwise landed whimsy. Cheval's was no dilettante production; it was a working-man's quest for meaning, and if it could be described as 'naïve' it achieved, paradoxically, the kind of sophistication that often eludes the consciously sophisticated.

Read French novels of the decades leading up to Cheval's masterpiece, and you frequently encounter the stubborn provincial intent on conquering the capital. But Cheval had no knowledge of, or interest in, Paris. He was unaware of those great movements in art that we cluster together under the term post-impressionism. Art nouveau? The Palais Idéal shares some of the features of that movement – the representation of organic growth, the plant and animal forms that seem to defy their objectively static condition. Symbolism? Again, there's common territory – the hauntingly atmospheric nature of the building, both of its parts and of its whole: if, as Walter Pater maintained, all art aspires to the condition of music, Cheval's Palais Idéal is 'Symbolist' inasmuch as it is art aspiring to the condition of dream – except that the terms 'Art nouveau' and 'Symbolist' would have meant nothing to Cheval, and his case was rather that of dream aspiring to the condition of art.

The Palais Idéal is a meeting place of the various arts, a powerfully integrative vision. It is sculpture as well as architecture, again as regards its constituent parts as well as its totality – a diversity-in-unity. It is theatre: your approach to it from the village, even via its custom-built entry-point, reveals a 'spectacle' in both the French and English meanings of that word. You reach the upper level of the Palais Idéal, by a choice of winding stairs, and find yourself on a terrace that suggests a stage – a stage that demands all France, and the world beyond, as its audience. It's also literature, for Cheval had a predilection for mottoes, scraps of poetry, and his own gnomic pronouncements, all of which he inscribed on his walls, not least those of the vaguely unnerving labyrinth - for so it is called - within the ground level of his eldritch castle:

> *Pour mon idée, mon corps a tout bravé,*
> *Le temps, la critique, les années.*
> *La vie est un rapide courrier,*
> *Ma pensée vivra avec ce rocher*

In itself it lacks one art: music. Even here, though, help is at hand – at least in the summer months when open-air performances take place in front of the monument.

The Palais Idéal has attracted the attention of later artists such as the Surrealists, for whom it became a place of pilgrimage: their Parisian equivalent would be the Buttes-Chaumont Park with its sinister caverns carved out of a former quarry. Antonio Gaudí is often plausibly compared with Cheval.

Two of the English-speaking world's most eloquent writers on art, Robert Hughes and John Berger, have come here and paid homage. Hughes has written of 'a palace of the unconscious' built by a 'proud and certain man'. Freud and Jung may indeed be hovering in and out of the structure, as well as Marx: Berger resists psychologising the work, preferring to stress the dialectical energies of the peasant-workman's interaction with his materials. (These materials, it should be added, are not only of stone – Cheval also collected and deployed shells, and sculpted with mortar: in his time he had worked as a baker, and kneading the dough proved itself to be a transferable skill.)

I suggested to the students in my aesthetics class at Grenoble that architecture was the one art you couldn't escape: it was all around you. Moreover, rather than you containing it, it contained you. Music might enter your body; your body must inevitably enter a building. Berger rightly maintains that books and even films about the Palais Idéal can never be a substitute for actually being there and inside it: 'You do not *look* at it any more than you look at a forest. You either enter it or you pass it by.' Nevertheless, as well as the books, I showed a DVD of it to my students: such a medium could reach the parts (of the building, and of human sensibility) that the best books couldn't reach. The new technology could at least offer an appetiser for the original's three-dimensionality; when I lectured on Cheval in my art college and evening class days, I had only slides to hand. Yet these images, for all their inadequacy,

were what led me to explore this monument in all its
existential palpability, this seemingly unlikely creation
of the dour postman of Hauterives.

Tom Hubbard
Grenoble/ Kirkcaldy 2013

PROLOGUE: SCOTLAND

THE RETOUR O TROILUS

The Testament of Cresseid *by Robert Henryson (c. 1420-c.1490) is my favourite Scottish poem. Despite its ultimate origins in Greek mythology and the Trojan War, the love story of Troilus and Cresseid belongs to mediaeval romance. Henryson's poem is a sequel (though it's much more than that) to Chaucer's* Troilus and Criseyde, *but it tells the tragic story with the focus on the lady and often from her point of view. Its most memorable lines, for me as for many, come during the famous 'recognition' scene. Here, the Trojan prince Troilus, victorious (temporarily) over the Greeks, encounters a gaunt beggar emerging from a leper-house:*

> Than upon him scho kest up baith her ene
> And with ane blenk it come into his thocht
> That he sumtime hir face befoir had sene.
> Bot scho was in sic plye he knew hir nocht;
> Yit than hir luik into his mynd it brocht
> The sweit visage and amorous blenking
> Of fair Cresseid, sumtyme his awin darling.

Has she really come to this? My sequel to the 'sequel', as it were, takes a retrospective look, from the perspective of a matured Troilus.

As a Fifer I'm especially proud of Dunfermline's own makar. That fine scholar of mediaeval Scottish literature, Matthew

11

McDiarmid, claimed that Henryson was the greatest tragic poet between Dante and Shakespeare.

I was the chairperson of the Robert Henryson Society from 2002 to 2005. During this period we held a Henryson Supper at Dunfermline's Abbot House, the second of its kind but the first in Scotland. Why should Burns get all the attention?

THE RETOUR O TROILUS

Ill-thriven laund, eenou ti me sae dear,
Cauldrife and courin frae the daithlie drow:
Lang-cowpit waas, ower mony ghaists ablow;
And yit I mynd the bluid-reid wine flowed here.

Why suid my youth feel auncient as thir stanes,
Why suid my prieven virr sae faa frae me,
Why suid my een, aye vieve efter the years
O cruellest scenes o fechtin, cryne frae this sicht?
Here at the burn that mirrors me throu time
I leuk upon mysel as yince I wis,
Like faither ti a son, leevin ti daid,
The past o Troy and Troilus. In this glen
I cam late ti manheid: she, the forehand
O aa the queans that ti my breist hae won,
The rare Cresseid; she, whase flichterin hairt
Felt delicat as ony timorsome mavie
That liltit ower oor heids; she, whase quick muivement
In guidin me ti a neuk, wis sib ti the con
Wha derts athort the pad, then vainishes …
Here at the saicret crag upon whase brou
Oor forefowk biggit the dun and steidit Troy,
We were twa glaikit bairns: the merest smitches
That an ever-twynin linn
Kests on the seg as, tentless, it hauds forrit.
Aye bydes the auld Troy fir Troilus. In this cave
A queen made her orisons, and we oor luves;
Whaur nou it's daurk, then glintit my leman's een,
Whaur nou it's foustie, then fufft her body's scent,
Whaur nou hing cobwabs, she cleikit me in her hair.

Thon wis the folly that first made me wyce,
Chynged the heich-heidit halflin wha kent aa

13

- Or sae he thocht – aboot the coorse o the state,
The macklike policies o peace and weir,
Wha laucht at ither men whase caa ti airms
Wis ti the airms o a mere paramour:
This wis your Troilus, buirdliest chiel o the land,
The rival o the gods, and no yit twinty!
I staun the-day, at the hinner-end o youth,
Amang the wrack o a kinrik and its fowk:
Ithers hae peyed mair dearlie nor mysel
Fir weavin o mishanter and mistak,
That skufft us frae oor umwhile eminence
Ti the untentit airts ayont the port:
Rickle o bleckened banes i the aise-midden
Or gruggilt beauty i the lazar-houss …

Cuid I but see the thristin o new life
Up throu the cleevin o the palace flair,
Ti spreid o emerant in the simmer sun –
Yit I maun leave, and come here nevermair.

But I can hear this ferlie: a deid-bell.
There's mair come back ti murn here nor mysel,
Aa wabsters, and the last o their trade in Troy,
In slaw processioun:
Yin o their feres is ti be yirdit süne.
Nane sall gang pairt o the road and then gie ower,
Nane but sall cairry the corp, or else attend it,
Ti the kirkyaird aa the wey.
                              Abüne us nou
The crummlin temple floats upon the haar.

Ower mony ghaists, fir me ti gang my lane;
Ower mony ghaists, the kinrik's, and my ain.

1985

14

BELGIUM

EUROPEAN CAPITAL

Since boyhood I've been fascinated by the 'oriental' architectural curiosities located at the north-western edge of greater Brussels. They're in the proximity of the lush public parklands – and the private royal domain – of Laeken. It was King Léopold II, impressed by the chinoiserie *and* japonaiserie *of the Paris Exhibition, who had them constructed in his capital. Since I wrote the following poem, the Chinese Pavilion and Japanese Tower have been opened to the public, and you can view superb collections of porcelain, carvings and other works of art and artefacts. Then you think of how Léopold came by the loot which funded your agreeable experience. Cue another look at the Congo-related writings of Mark Twain, Joseph Conrad and others – especially* The King Incorporated: Leopold the Second and the Congo *(1963; reprinted 1999) by the Scottish historian and journalist Neal Ascherson.*

At Laeken you encounter a case study in the relationship between aesthetics and ethics.

EUROPEAN CAPITAL

You were so innocent, loving the incongruous;
So thrawnly eager to reach some ill-known corner,
Some destination left unvisited
By all, it seemed, except your younger self …

The tram rattled, its bell ting'd
Its solo in the city's orchestra;
You were fifteen, exhilarated, foolish.
Did you remark, however fleetingly,
Looming before the bridge on the canal,
Those sculptural figures bearing the name of 'Labour'?
Your head rattled with darting images
Of silent nineteenth century legacy:
Avenue after avenue of mansions,
And the murky green of unlit lamps in file
That followed the high fencing of a park
Dour as the night;
The tram lurched, and from another angle
The city spread its serendipitous riches
That shimmered in the April afternoon.

You were so innocent, loving the incongruous,
So thrawnly eager to reach that ill-known corner
Where most rushed by on the way to somewhere else.
There were the objects of your pilgrimage:
Chinese pavilion, Japanese pagoda,
You'd quite ignore in China or Japan,
Bordering the suburbs and the palace grounds.
You were fifteen, exhilarated, foolish,
Unmindful of that larger Royal Domain
South of the alps, the sea, the desert, jungle,

From where the king and his go-getting minions
Extracted growth of ivory and rubber
And blood … so here, he makes his due return,
His tribute to all folk without white skins,
In raising up such droll exotica.

And yet, today, they're fousty and forgotten.
No longer here, at the dragons and lanterns,
No longer here, nor king nor belle époque.
Now, most rush by on the way to somewhere else,
And you … you followed them down a tentacle
Back to the swill and rumble of our time,
The towering blocks that snatch the very sky:
Cacophonous centre of one continent
That sucks and spews the centre of another.

Not that you saw that then, and barely now –
Through streets where everything and everyone
Seem fabricated just a minute ago –
Could you connect such serendipitous riches
With muffled protestations near at hand
Or flies and skeletons in a darker land.

You remain innocent, faced with the incongruous.

1986

FRANCE

BERLIOZ AT MEYLAN
EDGAR POE

The following poem grew out of an odd and fortunate combination of circumstances. In August 1992 the Scottish Arts Council awarded me a writer's bursary to work on Faustian themes in various forms – poetry, prose, drama – and a month later I was offered a six-month contract as a visiting lecturer at the Stendhal University of Grenoble. A few weeks before I set off for France, I visited my friend the composer and pianist Ronald Stevenson, who told me that I was heading for a very Faustian part of Europe; the composer of La damnation de Faust, *he informed me, had been born at La Côte-Saint-André, to the west of Grenoble.*

Grenoble itself was the birthplace of the novelist Stendhal, whose best-known novel, Le rouge et le noir, *is not without its Faustian resonances, as when its protagonist, the young Julien Sorel, experiences an epiphany on a mountain-top, and there are numerous references to Mephistopheles (indeed the novel itself operates between the poles of Faustian expansiveness and Mephistophelean irony). 'Had Stendhal written a symphony', wrote the music critic Ernest Newman, 'it would have been very like* Harold in Italy *[why not the* Symphonie fantastique? *- TH]; had Berlioz gone in for the novel he would have produced something like* Le rouge et le noir'.

The Stendhal University helped me find a place to stay: this turned out to be a résidence in the nearby commune of Meylan, where Berlioz had spent much of his boyhood at his maternal grandfather's house, and where he fell in love – at the age of twelve – with implications for the future Symphonie fantastique. *My Sunday walks (or rather climbs) must have retraced those of the young Berlioz. Since then, I've been able to 'hear' that mountainous landscape in his music.*

Eighteen years passed, and I returned to Grenoble as Professeur invité for the fall semester of 2011-12. Now, in the internet age, I was able to locate Berlioz's grandfather's house, and again clambered about the ruined 'Scottish' tower high above the village. This time I was staying in Grenoble itself, but Meylan was within walking distance of the campus. It seemed mellower, but then I myself was mellower.

BERLIOZ AT MEYLAN

1. Stella Montis

Look closely at the small silent one
With the big noise inside him.
Speak to him; - he averts his dark eyes,
Mutters fretfully, impatiently.
There is a party at his grandfather's house,
There is laughter in every room and in the garden.
The swish of the skirts, too much, too much:
His collar tightens, he must outside.

Under his favourite tree, he reads Cervantes.
He finds comfort in the faithful fuddled Don.
They would shake their heads, his elders, smilingly,
- With a gentle warning, perhaps,
If they knew the turn of his thoughts.
He is a knight of the rocky glen:
He halts his steed by the spring
Hears voices from the ruined tower –
'Poor Hector! His head is full of Walter Scott!'

So the dream breaks, brutally, as always.
Is that his uncle, and the sound of his spurs,
Is that his uncle, dancing with *her*?
Oh, the anguish of a boy of twelve
Gazing at a woman of eighteen!
And then the game, and the taking sides:
Each cavalier must choose his partner.
The boy blushes, he cannot hide.
'I'll choose', she says, and sparkles near to him.
'This is my beau – let me present to you
My own Monsieur Hector.'

Quivering in the nest,
The future eagle of the alps
Is a tiny, wounded lark.

2. Nocturne

It is cool on the heights of Meylan.
Two women recline on marble;
One questions, the other replies,
Their voices join in the evening quiver.

- *Vous soupirez, madame?*

Beyond, across the valley,
The moon brings forth the mountain snows; the chain
Of Belledonne looms through the mise-en-scène
Of the challenged ones: who brood with troops of
                              friends
Marching between rocks and lakes, hoping, expecting
The gates of Grenoble, opened; … and those, more
                              prey than eagle,
Who dodge in cave and cellar
Getting the message (and the men) through, the
                              women as brave and braver,
Watchful throughout the passion of the times
For that merely changing gesture of a comrade
That leads at last to death at the roadside wall:
Casting their blood, where, later, children lay flowers
- Yet a loved lady bemoans her heavy hours!

- *Quoi! Vous pleurez, madame?*

Yes, weeping for empires, pacts, betrayals.

The moon brings forth, over the terrace,
The statue of a mother and son:
Two women recline on marble;
One questions, the other replies.

3. *Le rouge et le noir*

With the energy of Faust
With the laughter of Mephistopheles
The man of the rocks
Is scornful of Paris,
Frigid, effete
- Though Harriet played there!

Poor Harriet, perfervid Celt,
As Juliet, Ophelia,
Revealed all Shakespeare
To the amorous Dauphinois.

('Romanticism pleases French Shakespeareans,
But Classicism pleases their great-grandads.'
And Metropolitanism's
For Metropoltroons.)

Ah! If only the harshness
Between Hector and Harriet
Had never been more
Than the crazy raillery
Between Béatrice and Bénédict:

And yet … no pistol-shot,
As when Julien Sorel
Felled Madame de Rênal:
Hector ascends not the scaffold
But more familiar slopes;

His head has been greying
With earlier hopes.

Hector, dark wanderer,
Again to Meylan bound,
With all his love's labours
Not lost, but unfound.

4. *Ripeness is All*

Having pursued his Damnation
Across Europe,
In Breslau, Passau,
Vienna, Pest;
Leaving his bed, in Prague,
Writing in the middle of the night
The apotheosis of Marguérite:

> *'Remonte au ciel, âme naïve*
> *Que l'amour égara.'*

Having called up demons
From the orchestra pit,
Tones that before
Were uncombined, unheard;
Magic at court for every Emperor
Except the chancer of the Tuileries,
Whose alchemists are borrowed from the Bourse;
Having soothed, stirred or scorned
The ears of Europe:
For him, *the insubstantial pageant faded*
Leaves not a rack behind …he seeks the stone,
The stone where once Estelle, taking his hand,
Had crossed the mountain stream. Here, his true voice
Unites itself, as ever,

To forests, crags and torrents; heights of Meylan,
So much in place a quarter-century on,
Save that Estelle has gone –

- To Lyon.

See him, now, at sixty-one,
Only a few years remaining to him;
Not as far-gone as Lear, but certainly
A fond foolish old child, who 'is not reasonable';
(Neither sane, nor insane, but a-sane …)
'We shall meet', she writes. 'after my son's wedding;
I am very touched by your feelings … all these years.'

He is the happiest of hosts to Estelle's boy
And his bride:
This Prospero finds a Ferdinand and Miranda.

The return to life: but the last episodes
In the life of the artist. Hector seeks Estelle
Now in Geneva. Walks by the lakeside gardens,
The steamers both absorbing and emitting
Assorted English burghers, with toy-wives;
Here a Falstaff, much more sober, still as fat;
There a Caliban, with his top hat and cane.

Hector proposes, and Estelle declines.
They look to Mont Salève; perhaps their thoughts
Are further south … to Meylan: there, too early,
And here, too late, too late …

1993

Hold on – this is the French section: why the following poem on an American writer? It's because of Poe's cult status in France, where his work has been appreciated in a manner very different from its reception in America and other 'Anglo-Saxon' countries.

It all goes back to Charles Baudelaire's admiration for Poe; his French translations of the American's short stories remain the standard classic versions (Stéphane Mallarmé did the same for Poe's poetry). Baudelaire shared Poe's mysterious, Gothic sensibility, with its love of the macabre, and awareness of the artist as exile. The two writers also had in common stepfathers whom they loathed; in an act of solidarity, Baudelaire dropped the name of Poe's stepfather, John Allan. Since then the American writer has always been known in France as Edgar Poe.

Baudelaire was indignant at the way in which – according to him – Poe was variously despised and neglected in his native land. Baudelaire felt particular ire for the critic Rufus Griswold, whom he accused of trashing Poe's posthumous reputation: why, demanded Baudelaire, are dogs allowed into American cemeteries? As his poetry often demonstrates, Baudelaire was a great cat lover. Perhaps American culture is essentially canine, as French is feline.

The Symbolist movement in France can trace its pedigree to 'Edgar Poe' via Baudelaire. Maurice Rollinat (1846-1903) was a French poet very much in the Baudelairean mode; he belonged to a group called Les Hydropathes, who refused to drink water, always preferring wine or beer. Rollinat and his confrères were performers at the renowned Montmartre cabaret, Le Chat Noir.

EDGAR POE

From the French of Maurice Rollinat

He was all demon, no angel he of God:
No nightingale, his song was of the crow;
And in the diamond of the wicked and the odd
He graved his elegant nightmares. Edgar Poe

Sought in the abyss, where all that's sane fragments,
Secrets of death and of eternity,
And his soul, which lit the bloody lineaments
Of crime, revealed the imp of perversity.

Chaste, mysterious, sardonic, and ferocious,
He refines the intense, he sharpens the atrocious;
His tree's a cypress; his wife, a ghost.

Before his lynx's eye, behold the answér:
Ach! How I comprehend why Baudelaire
Loved the Great Dark you read there, chilled, engrossed!

2012

SPAIN

EL GRECO TOWNSCAPE

I visited Toledo, long after I wrote these lines, in the course of a research trip to Spain; until then, my visual image of the city was derived from the paintings of El Greco. However, I had also been working on a short book about Michael Scot (c. 1175-c. 1235), the Scottish polymath who had based himself in Toledo, where he oversaw the translation of Arabic scientific texts into Latin. During the Middle Ages scientists were regarded as wizards, in league with the devil, and Scot became the subject of many legends. Dante consigns him to one of the circles of the **Inferno**. *I see him as yet another Faust-type.*

Toledo was once noted as a centre of religious toleration. When I was there, I was able to visit a cathedral, a synagogue and a mosque within a short space and in a single day.

EL GRECO TOWNSCAPE

Toledo!
A spectre-city, blanching the ridge to strange horizons,
Drawing in the moonlight to its bare stone;
Yielding and resisting with equal pride,
Quivering over the scorched sand, the cascading glen;
The glower of the night dissolves into flecks of pink
Over the wall-towers to the citadel:
Toledo takes on flesh
As by a miracle.

1993

ITALY

POMPEII
PAOLO TO FRANCESCA
CATULLUS LXI
LA MADRE DEI LAGHI

'Pompeii' was composed during a period of Cold War tension. Reagan and Thatcher were in power, and there was no prospect of change in the Soviet Union and its satellite states – until, that is, the emergence of Mikhail Gorbachev in 1985, but that was just the start of unforeseeable developments. At the time I was an active member of CND (the Campaign for Nuclear Disarmament).

POMPEII

The leevin enter at the lang-deid yett;
The leevin enter, but they winna byde:
Naebody bydes here nou. They'll pey their debt
O brief remembrance o a brief aside
They leared at schuil. They hae aareadies peyed
Their tickets, and are satisfied they came.
The leevin enter, but they'll gang back hame.

They've come, juist nou, frae sic a muckle steir
O modren weys, life at a constant jolt;
The like ne'er kent sin fou twa thousan year
Whan aa within thir waas cam ti a halt:
Yit it wis thrang eneuch, this muckle vault
That yince had been a toun, and nou stauns bare;
That yince had been a toun, and is nae mair.

This is a day unlike thon weirdit day:
Sic chiels as us, we ken it's no oor last.
It's bricht atween Vesuvius and the bay
Like life itsel, and ilka day that's passed
Wi ilka day that's yit ti come, can cast
Nae mirk the nou. Why tremble fir whit waits
By the intersection o thae drumlie gates?

This is a day maist like thon weirdit day:
Sic chiels as us, they tuik their dauner here,
Blethered, slockened a drouth, nae thocht ti spae
Gin they wad see the morn; and cuid ye speir
The warkin fowk, they'd hae nae cause ti fear
But that they'd sweit and trauchle, still and on,
Their buiths still thrang wi wasters whan they'd gone.

And there were luvers here, whase daffin words
Birled on the sooch that straiks us luvers nou;
Their sang taen up by foontains and by burds,
Gin aa that muives had come this wey ti woo.
But somethin muived ayont, and frae the mou
O the muckle ben, this gentle land itsel
Spewed furth the horrors o a crimson hell.

Sall we wha visit here withoot a thocht
O bein yirdit sae untimeous-like,
Sall we traverse thir doolie strachts, and nocht
Depairt at last ayont the city's dyke
Uncheenged? Sall we again mak sic a fyke
O aa the fatuous wheegees o oor time?
The past's disaster is the future's crime.

This scene wis nature's wark, it wisna man's,
But nature's been oot-rivalled some while back:
Hiroshima – Nagasaki – aa oor plans
Ti prieve there's nane like us wha hae the knack.
Vesuvius – huh! See whit it failed ti wrack –
Thir fancy pentins and siclike were safe.
Gie us the chaunce, and we'll ding doun the lave!

Fir siccarlie we wadna leave ahent
Ane single objeck that cuid tell the tale –
Muild o a dug richt frae his maister rent,
Muild o a quean wha bields ti nae avail.
Naethin ti tell – ti naebody! Wad the wale
O fowk still leevin, gin that ony be,
Feel sae uptaen bi archaeology?

33

There's desolation aither side o the waa.
Nae faur frae here, there's puirtith and there's skaith.
The leevin tak their gate, fir they've seen aa
Pompeii can offer. Yit a hint o braith
Can still be felt frae this dreich neuk o daith:
Look there, i the airt o the ben, and mark that faun
Dauncin as gin he were alive. Daunce on!

1984

The following sonnet is an attempt at variations on one of the great stories of doomed lovers. A number of Scottish poets have made versions of Dante, in whole or in part, including Byron (who translated this particular episode into English), together with Tom Scott and W.S. Milne, whose work in Scots is warmly recommended. Painters and composers have also been attracted to this tragic tale; one example is Rakhmaninov's deeply affecting one-act opera Francesca da Rimini *of 1904-5.*

PAOLO TO FRANCESCA

(Dante, *Inferno*, Canto V)

Villages sliced down the middle by a wall;
Neighbours waving to each other through the stark
Bounds of barbed wire, ploughed strip, watchtower
                                        and all
That parts convivial lights, demands the dark;
Exiles whose passion calls as it must call,
Crackling through lines that unwelcome listeners
                                        mark;
The smuggled notes between those who can scarcely
                                        crawl,
Like cast-out tykes who have yet some bite and bark.
They are nobler far than me, and shall connect
In the years to come, when this my gentle rage
Is lost with the rager: gentle, but guilty too.
They shall endure, the innocent elect,
In such a union that, as you turn the page,
I by your side may never know with you.

1986

On its first publication in an anthology, Liz Lochhead singled out the next piece for comment. Catullus belonged to what is now Sirmione at the southern end of Lake Garda.

CATULLUS LXI

Pit by the time fir bydin:
  By Venus you are blest.
  Hit's clear ti ilka guest
Whit force steirs groom and bride in
A luve that's no fir hidin.

Wha numbers the sands o Afrikie
  Or the glisterin stars their names,
Wad find mair trauchle gin that he
Ettled ti tot up eidently
  Your mony-thoosand randy games.

Pley weill, mak luve, lat your flesh mell
That it perpetuates itsel:
  Sic bonny young folk as you are
  Honour your forefolk when you gar
Your growthie bodies rise and swell.

Lassies, sneck the yett:
  The jiggin's ower, we're awa hame,
But you, newly conjoinit,
  Big braw lad and sonsie dame:
You'll pairty on through life, I'll bet.

2004

At the end of a lecture tour of northern Italy in January 1996, I spent a few days in Como, which I had not visited since childhood. I took a bus and train from there to Campione on Lake Lugano. Walking through this Italian enclave, which is surrounded by Swiss territory, I entered a small church and heard the water lapping on the shore. I am not a Catholic, but my family was so in previous generations; one feels, at least, a cultural connection. This is also one of many poems either inspired by the Alps, or composed in their vicinity.

'Paradiso' is the name of the southern part of the Swiss city of Lugano.

LA MADRE DEI LAGHI
(The Mother of the Lakes)

Here, a strange room. Your papers lie unpacked.
At last, you are alone. The classroom fades:
But your own phantom youth is unrelaxed,
To haunt you down the shadows of arcades.

The mirror, and your mother's grey-blue eyes
Look out through thirty years. You both came here,
She younger than you now. – *What children's cries*
To you unknown, who never felt their fear?

She nursed you through. The little boy in Como
Laughed in the sun: you were freed northerners;
That market-stall in the Piazza del Duomo –
You ate your share of the orange, and then hers.

The campanile swung and creaked each hour
That brought you back to Italy to teach.
You draw from students your imparted power,
Explaining a point in (somewhat) of their speech.

You laugh with them, hiding the miracle
That where you toddled, so today you stride.
Their parents age with you. – By the arch, hold still:
Never forget the little ones who died.

From breasts of rock, from Europe's endless whites:
From lake that bears or buries, you recall
Your infant sleep, while Campione's lights
Were chugged far off: the boat's own barcarolle

That set you dreaming, huddled on the deck,
Lulled off to Paradiso under stars:
Less mindful of the hand that stroked your neck
Than of Swiss chocolate, toy funiculars,

Then waking in a room to wonder how
You got there – all the lapping dark between
That shore, and this – just as you lumber now,
Suddenly graceless in a shrinking scene.

Desperate gentlenesses: so you seek
For random fellows across continents,
For you have smelt an ever-thickening reek
Smother our last vestigial innocence,

Even as it shone anew: oh dearest young,
For whom our guidance is that ancient rite
As to an alpine goddess we have sung,
Our common cradle sinking in the night.

1996

GERMANY

In its original form, what follows is one of Brecht's best-known pieces; there are many English versions, and I thought it was time to have one in Scots.

SPEIRINS

From the German of Bertolt Brecht

Wha biggit the seiven yetts o Thebes?
The buiks are stecht wi the names o kings.
Wis kings the boys that rugged up aa thae
                               boulders?
And Babylon, that aften wracked,
Wha had ti pit the hale jing-bang thegither?

In whit kinna hooses
O gowdblinterin Lima, bade thae that wrocht it?
At lowsin-time, whan they'd feenished the
                               Cheenese waa,
Whaur gaed the masons?

Muckle Rome is fu
O 'triumphal' airches.
Wha biggit thaim? Forby
Ower wha were the Caesars 'triumphal'?

Then Byzantium, that aa thir sangs are aboot,
Had it nocht but palaces fir aa its fowk?

Even in Atlantis o the tales,
The nicht the sea engowfed it,
The drounin maisters raired oot fir their sclaves.

That lawdie Alexander conquessed Indie …
Aa his lane?
Caesar licked the Gauls …
Had he no even a cuik wi him?
Philip o Spain grat
As his fleet gaed unner.

Did naebody else greet?
Frederick the Saicont won the Seiven Year Weir.
Wha won it tae?

Ilka page a victory.
Wha cuiked the victory banket?

Ilka year some heid-bummer.
Wha peyed up?

That mony reports.

That mony speirins.

1988

The next poem has its setting in Germany, to the west of Koblenz, in a region which is dominated by the vast twelfth-century monastery church of Maria Laach, a magnificent example of Romanesque architecture. It's also an area of former volcanic activity, and the lake (which the church overlooks) is almost perfectly round in outline. My father loved this place and, some months after his death, I took my own son there. The poem draws on childhood memories of a quiet corner a few kilometres to the south-east of the church.

LAACHERSEE ELEGY

*By the Erntekreuz, SE of the Abbey Church
of Maria Laach, in the direction of Mendig,
Rheinland-Pfalz, Germany*

Son, I am taking you to your grandfather's
Loved landscapes, for the year of his death is falling:
Young you stride through the yellow fields at the
                                                   lakeside,
Now following me, now leading me up the brae
To the volcanic outcrop where I played
When I was half your age. Late afternoon bells,
    Suggestion of unheard toccata of Bach
    Reach me alone from the Maria Laach.

I was the boy on that explorable mound,
    Its paths now disappearing in the bramble;
I am the man who scarce believes he's found
    Its paths leading within him. Now I stumble
When you call me, Chris, as my parents called me
                                                   down
To take our piece. My own ghost whistles on:
    I have been here before, I know that true,
    But feel a weirdness as of déjà vu.

I have been here before:
    All that has been, recurs,
Theme, with variations,
As I can't regain the summit of the tor
    But scrunch the twigs around, nettles and burrs:
I'll take my seat between the generations,
    My Chris on one side, blethering away;
    And my dad, when gazing toward the Laachersee.

47

Beyond the track, the rising forest-patch
  With its wayside shrine, half-hidden, madonna and
                                    child:
Here I trace back the crouched eleven-year-old,
  Drawing with earnest line the faded figures
In his bumper German sketch-book. Nothing at all
To show you, Chris, of my last innocent scrawl
  Before looming rigours. You take the camera,
  To reinstate my lost ephemera.

The basalt cross which welcomes folk to rest
  Is carved with prayer for daily bread and wine;
 Abandoned faith, once echoing down our line:
Yet we can praise those who provided.
Winter, Frühling, Sommer, Herbst;
Winter, Spring, Simmer, Hairst.
  I silently invoke our absent one,
  But it's my own voice that answers: *Son.*

2004

Schellbronn is a small town to the north-west of Stuttgart. I was recalling a mellow, late-summer evening during the 1970s. The symphony was Alexander von Zemlinsky's Second, to which I'd been introduced at the time: not the most apt piece of music, perhaps, but apt enough for me.

SCHELLBRONN

Gloamin. Fore-end o August, ten year syne.
Lythe wis the air ayont the clachan-fuit
Whaur I laid by, and leukit ti the line
O trees that daurkened ti the verra ruit.
There, at the mairch o the loan, mirk wad meet mirk:
Man's yird that maun gie ower the day's stramash,
The lift that recks na o his ilka fash,
Fir aa his blethers i the howff or kirk.
Yit I that nicht saw miracles heich abüne,
As reid ti crimson melled, richt braisantlie,
Purpie, then black, ti lang await the dawn.
I warsle still ti hark at whit I'd seen,
That wis ane muivement o a symphony,
And there is mair ti hear afore I'm gone.

1985

SWITZERLAND

THE TERRACE AT BASEL
AN ANTIQUARIAN PRINT
FRAE *VOCATIOUN O THE RIVERS*

A favourite Matthew Arnold poem, from his sequence 'Switzerland', is 'The Terrace at Berne', which has these haunting lines: 'Like driftwood spars which meet and pass / Upon the boundless ocean-plain, / So on the sea of life, alas! / Man nears man, meets, and leaves again.' Basel's terrace, like Bern's, is next to the cathedral and overlooks the river. Basel, however, is a frontier city, and such cities tend to have a particular historical significance. Dostoyevsky came here, as recorded in his wife's diary; in more recent times, the German artist Joseph Beuys (1921-86) participated in the city's spring carnival. Beuys also made a significant mark on the Edinburgh arts scene during the 1970s, via the good offices of Richard Demarco and his co-workers. The Goetheanum at Dornach, to the south-east of Basel, is the centre of the Rudolf Steiner movement: its 'organic' architecture is akin to art nouveau, but its style derives from Goethe's writings, not least those on the growth of plants. The Scottish composer Ronald Stevenson has performed at the Goetheanum with a programme of music based on Faustian themes. All these elements are interrelated.

THE TERRACE AT BASEL

- And witness those who rendezvous
At this rampart above the Rhein;
Twin spires assertive to the flow
Of nations mingling at the line,

And as the Munster's shadow on your face
Restrains the kiss once summoned by the sun,
Let us smile sadly with discovered grace
For every flower placed inside a gun.

We seek no drama for this common stage,
No fall of gods, no full blood-quickening cup,
Nor lakeside idyll from another age:
Just the recurrent nocturne wafting up.

Others met here, no doubt, amazed
That they'd survived to meet at all;
One younger, stumbling, faintly crazed –
One older, welcoming, by the wall.

Now couples amble by the parapet's
Vista of history and its regrets:
Across the bridges, in green finery,
The trams ply between France and Germany.

A Russian prophet and his lady here
Rested, as folk criss-crossed the gravel plain:
The palimpsest long written, year by year,
By those protected from the encircling pain –

And so this bearded gambler, fretting, ill,
Enslaved by chance, embattled with free will,
Found in this town an image of his lot:
Christ's corpse, blessed by a princely idiot.

Below, the town insouciantly chats.
A sculpture shakes, spins, cranks its water-wheels
And joky levers. Through Barfüsserplatz
A spring procession to a drum-beat reels.

A bony clown, be-cloaked, with his felt hats,
Once grinned it on; his carnival causerie
Challenged the new quotidian autocrats.
The trams ply between France and Germany,

Undulating almost with elegance
The steeps and narrows of the centre:
Relentless screeching eloquence,
Scheduled anarchic adventure.

Compact of puritan and libertine,
This is a land for us, though not our own,
My fellow pilgrim; Switzerland has been
Guiltily centred and yet too alone

From vaster guilts: it filters, concentrates
Diverse elixirs from its neighbouring states,
Absorbing, sometimes blending: the essence
Of carefully manufactured innocence.

But here's a space that's sanctioned for a show
Of polyglottal metamorphoses,
Where masks unmask, the resurrected grow
Through this hard continent's interstices.

Then looking south to Dornach, even we
Plying between gates and states mechanically
Can our old selves unclock, be nurtured still
In tree-like temples rising from the hill.

2000

Louis Duchosal (1862-1901) was a prominent French-writing Swiss poet associated with the Symbolist movement. One wouldn't readily link Calvinist Geneva with Symbolism, which seems closer to Catholic culture, and which in any case has a reputation for the outrageous and the erotic. Decadence is at odds with piety; but one could argue that Calvinism offers a dark, doom-laden perspective which accords with Symbolism's morbidity. It's also advisable not to identify Calvinism too absolutely with puritanism. Duchosal is a poet in the Baudelairean mode – see also Rollinat's 'Edgar Poe' above – and indeed it was James Robertson's versions of Baudelaire which led me to suggest to my Scottish confrère that he have a go at Duchosal. The superb results are in James's pamphlet Hem and Heid (Kettillonia, 2009). After reading his Duchosal versions at a Swiss poetry reading in Edinburgh, James remarked: 'If that's not Swiss Symbolism, I don't know what is.'

Duchosal's work is absent from the bookshops of Geneva and Lausanne, even the second-hand ones. You can download a few poems from the internet, and that's about it, apart from selections in anthologies which are not easy to come by. However, in that cavernous used bookstore in a courtyard behind Geneva's main train station, I was able to track down a monograph on the poet's friend, the Bernese-Genevan painter Ferdinand Hodler, and this contains generous quotations from Duchosal's journalistic writings. Like Baudelaire before him, Duchosal was an art critic as well as a poet.

AN ANTIQUARIAN PRINT

From the French of Louis Duchosal

A welter here of sounds, of lights and wings,
And the scents floating of lily and orange-tree;
There's a young girl advancing gracefully,
Her bonnet with bright asphodels as trimmings.

A troupe of children, loving nudity,
Frolic in the river at resplendent dawn:
Innocent laughter's languorously borne
Like incense, to the carmine of the sky.

Spring bids us join her sublime revelling;
- But, in the grass, the ivy twists, reveals
A musty, grinning skull. Down there, one feels,
Death sets his stroke upon the scene of the living.

2001

In the course of a Swiss poetry project which engaged me during the early 2000s, I was in touch with the veteran French-writing poet Maurice Chappaz (1916-2009); his correspondence (as indeed his poetry) suggested a thoroughly decent and gentle man. There was a steely side, however: he was a public figure who, coming from an area of great natural beauty, spoke out on human responsibility toward the environment. His long poem, Vocation des fleuves, *belongs as much to the western Alpine and Mediterranean region generally as to his own canton of Valais – belongs indeed to our threatened world, and my hope is that it will continue to find its way into other languages. I would call this work a 'praise-poem' – to use a concept from Scottish Gaelic tradition.*

FRAE *VOCATIOUN O THE RIVERS*

From the French of Maurice Chappaz

I hae on my tongue a snaw-flaucht and unner my
                                    dowp a brennin flint
I lauch
The Valais i my harns whyles is sib ti Norway sib ti
                                    Brittany sib ti Provence
A gairden i Provence a desert i Spain
Whit are lift and nicht daein thegither?
And whit are the starns bringin furth i the brainches
                                    o the larick?
I jalouse a heich glen in India
In aa relatiouns wi my fowk I'm tenty o muckle
                                    wee Judaea
The pink carnatioun o the craigs is mairrit on
                                    the prood white lily
Hit's the Jordan that steals inti the bed o the Rhône
The cathedrals are biggit the white leam o ilka
                                    brae-face hermitage
The chaipel skinkles
Like a drap o brandy on the gresslaund up the ben.

2001

AUSTRIA

MUSIC AT KUFSTEIN
ICEBERG

The massive Heldenorgel *can be seen – and heard – in the fortress of Kufstein, an Austrian town near the German border. If you approach the town after several hours hiking in the mountains, the effect is especially powerful. 'The wae o a wowf' hints at certain Freudian themes, and also at a more intimate (if often melancholy) genre in music – the Austro-German* Lied *of which Hugo Wolf (1860-1903) was a master. Wolf's creative life was cut short, five years before his corporeal death, by mental illness. 'Makar's touer' – a couple of years after I wrote this poem, I was guest-lecturing in Tübingen, where the poet Hölderlin was holed up in a turret for the last thirty-six years of his life.*

MUSIC AT KUFSTEIN

I heard the Alps echo my dule o the past year
Whan my warld and I were clanked in a nairra neuk,
Ti chowk upon the reek; whan my lugs were deaved
Bi jylers and jyled aye threipin, gleg to sook
The peeriest drap o peyson: we forgot
    Oor need fir an antidote.

That time cam back ti me i the Kaisergebirge,
Whaur the dungeon's dunner rose ti the thinnest
                                 skreek;
I lauched ti think mysel sib ti the earn
Wha wadna fash himsel upon his peak
Yit glisked ablow, and in that moment kent
    The weird o oor continent.

At that touerin tumeness, empires had aince met,
Syne riven apairt; the bens theirsels cheenge less,
And the map's reid line tweests anerlie on the map
That crummles süner: shairly this wilderness
Nae fowk cuid ever howp ti cultivate,
    But wad leave mair desolate?

I gaed doun bi the steps cut i the stane;
Wuids, burns, ferms, the thrang road ti the north
Aa birlin aneth my feet: shoogle o cells
Throu a microscope: but I cam fremmit forth
At last ti a toun, and a cheenge cam ower me then
    Like a god made man again.

He that's kest oot, and canna speir whit fir,
Wary o friens, and wary o himsel;
Wha's lowped frae the hotterin glaur ti the siccar rock –

But gin he'll find his saucht, he daurna tell;
He it is comes sudden, and bi chaunce,
  Ti tak haunds fir the daunce.

Sae I cam oot o a vennel inti the square
That filled wi organ-music frae abüne,
Dirlin inti howffs, or gurgin up the river
Ti Bavairie; sae afore that nicht wis düne,
Bach, Franz Schmidt, Beethoven, Bruckner and mair
  Tuik the simmer air.

Nae the wae o a wowf, dern in a forest o pipes,
Nor makar's touer that seals him frae the toun,
Nae grippy guaird o music's mystery
Cuid pairt the raible frae thon seilfu soun:
Kufstein's fortrace, aince dedicat ti weir,
  Bids aabody hear

That nou it lowses beauty raither nor bluid,
That ilka note suid raise a sodger's ghaist
Ti haunt a leevin hert. Rare instrument,
Biggit ti win us back frae Europe's waste;
Daily diapason, steirin my ain bit leid
  Itsel ti mak remeid.

1988

While still in her twenties, the Austrian poet and scholar Heidelinde Prüger (b. 1973) gained a following in Scotland with her book on the Perth makar William Soutar and her own versions of his poetry in Viennese dialect. She has also worked on Soutar's journals, has edited the work of another Perth poet, Alex Galloway, and produced other scholarly writings on Scottish literary, historical and cultural topics. Heidi and I have translated each other and presented our collaborations at a seminar at the University of Vienna.

This short lyric appealed to me partly – and perhaps oddly – because of Austrian landscapes, both actual and as represented in the arts (I used to teach a university course on Vienna 1900). Icebergs aren't a feature of this inland country, but I couldn't help thinking of a tiny boat rocking on a lake, an image which features in fin-de-siècle Austrian painting and in the poetry of Georg Trakl.

ICEBERG

From the German of Heidelinde Prüger

Quait, quait, my ben
harks in the sea o your thochts,
as the unsinkable brusts,
ti the tenderness o waves and ice.

2003

POLAND

The following poem grew out of a visit (or 'expedition' as it was called) by cultural workers, under the aegis of Edinburgh's Demarco Gallery, to Poland in the spring of 1989. We were there shortly before the partially-free elections which brought Solidarity to power. I saw the graveyard from the bus, which sped past; I had only a few moments to take in the scene.

CANDLES

Poznań-Wrocław, May 1989

The candles at the side of the road
Are flaring calmly, blazing softly;
Passion so purified in the dark
Of a tiny graveyard in a wood.
The candles looming through ribbons and flowers:
The dates of the dead upon the stones:
They've lain here longer than ever they lived,
Under the trees at the side of the road.

They've lain here longer than ever they lived,
All wartime people: parents, children;
We of their age, we who survived,
Visit this neuk at the highwayside:
Here is our family's last flitting,
From the rubble of the tenement,
From the laughter and anguish of our city
- But where were all the others sent?

The laughter and anguish of our city:
We dimly know it as it was.
Today, where the boulevards intersect,
The hoardings have no message for us.
The trams are clattering to the stance,
The kiosks sell their spring bouquets;
The folk criss-cross the pavement cracks
Where grass dries in the dust and haze.

The folk crush in and out of trams:
We dimly see in every face
Through weariness and wariness
The subtle lineaments, the trace

Of the centuries: the latent grace
That lit our lost ones in the wood,
Like candles by the highwayside
That flicker longer than they should.

The candles at the side of the road;
The wind drifts faintly through the trees;
The tears dissolve in the dark earth;
Elements of remembrances.
Yet there's a quickening of each name:
Its graven golds on whites and blacks
Vie with the leaping of the flame
Against the falling of the wax.

1989

HUNGARY

HIMNUSZ (1823)
RED HEDGEHOG
HAME THOCHTS, FRAE THE MED
BIRTHPLACE
THE PAINTER TIVADAR CSONTVÁRY

For the spring semester of 2006 I was a visiting professor in Scottish literature and culture at the Eötvös Loránd University of Budapest, on a Hungarian Government scholarship and a grant from the Scottish Arts Council. The latter funds enabled me to work on translations from Hungarian and also on an anthology, co-edited with Dr Zsuzsanna Varga, of Scottish poetry translated into Hungarian.

Another good friend and colleague, Dr Emília Szaffner, commissioned me to produce a Scots version of Kölcsey's 'Himnusz'. The original text is that of the Hungarian national anthem, for which the opera composer Ferenc Erkel supplied the music. We were able to have my version ready in time for Hungary's National Day (15 March), and Emi included it in her online scholarly journal, Epona, *which specialises in Scottish, Welsh and Irish studies.*

HIMNUSZ (1823)

From the Hungarian of Ferenc Kölcsey

God, bless the Magyar
  Wi blytheness and plenty,
Guaird this brave sodger
  At his maist tenty;
Oor weird has proven sair:
  God, cheer us in oor need,
Through aa that we maun bear
  Fir the past, and whit's aheid.

Oor forefolk You came guidin
  Ti the sacrit ben:
A hamelaund fir the bydin,
  Though won by bluid o men.
And by the reamin linn
  o Tisza, Danube, baith,
Árpád's braw-like efterkin
  Fared weill eneuch til daith.

You gien us the grain,
  Sweyin growthily:
You gien us the grape
  Nectar o Tokaj.
You hae plantit oor banner
  On the Turkish tumulus,
And the prood dun o Vienna
  Fell ti oor king, Mathias.

Syne we hae transgressed,
  That there's fire in Your hert,
And You hae shot fest
  Through the thunder, your dert,

Like the Tartars descendin
   Upon oor folk,
And oor lang years bendin
   Neath the Sultan's yoke.

Aftentimes we heard the rair
   o Ozman's murtherin gang:
Aroond the banes o brave men there
   They daunced their victory sang.
And aftentimes a Magyar's haund
   Tichtened a Magyar's noose,
And the son made o his mitherlaund
   His ain charnel-hoose.

The fugitive inby his cave
   Has dangers yit ti flee:
He looks aroond, and sees a grave
   Whaur his kintra suid be.
He's up the craig, and doun the glen,
   Wi nae a smitch o hope within him:
He sinks in dubs o bluid, and then
   Oceans o fire leap oot abüne him.

A great touer stuid here,
   At this cowp o stane:
Fine leddies and guid cheer,
   Whaur nou the wind maks mane.
Ah, freedom is a noble thing,
   Whan won withoot slauchter -
The lament that slaves sing,
   The orphaned son and dochter.

God, peety oor laund,
   Fir the blaws that we hae taen.
Guaird this brave baund

On the sea o their pain:
Oor weird has proven sair:
   God, cheer us in oor need,
Through aa that we maun bear
   Fir the past, and whit's aheid.

2006

The House of the Red Hedgehog (Vörös Sün Ház), formerly an inn, is located in the Castle quarter of Buda, at no. 3 András Hess Square. The original mediaeval building has been much renovated, but above one of the doors there survives a relief sculpture showing a hedgehog in a forest. During the eighteenth century, this was the house of Buda's first theatre: our hedgehog lingers as the star of the show, a real wee trouper as we'd say.

RED HEDGEHOG

In Budapest, up Castle Hill,
  You'll find yourself agog
To see him, snuffling, wary, still,
  My friend: the red hedgehog.

No fence, no fortress keeps him in,
  Nor are his foes kept out:
The spikes across his russet skin
  Quite nonchalantly sprout.

Reposing on his chalk-white field
  He's like a swollen log
All fungusy, its bark concealed –
  Ha! Cunning red hedgehog.

The stunted trees of his domain
  Shelter him well, no doubt;
To yield to hassle, he'd disdain
  With one snort of his snout.

When town and river and people all
  Have sunk into the bog,
Think of the sign upon the wall
  Of the Inn of the Red Hedgehog.

1998

A friend of the composers Bartók and Kódaly, who both made song-settings of his poetry, Endre Ady (1877-1919) was one of the major figures of Hungarian modernism. Like the composers, he found in French culture the perfect antidote to the Austro-German hegemony of the Hapsburgs, and remodelled traditional forms – such as the old Hungarian ballads – for a twentieth-century sensibility. He seems to have experienced a love-hate relationship with his native land, at once loathing those ways in which it allowed itself to become provincialised, and yearning to return there from his (enjoyable) French séjours. The resulting ironies are evident in these two poems, and are not unfamiliar to the socially-existentialist conflicts of expat Scots.

HAME THOCHTS, FRAE THE MED

From the Hungarian of Endre Ady

I'll no byde here upon my dowp,
Nor dump mysel here in the Med.
My cowp'll be a Magyar cowp.

Ach, at the edge o Transylvanie,
Ach, puir lamentit Hungary,
There, makar, dee: that laund'll ken ye.

Lang syne, he wis the braw young chancer,
But nou he's wabbit, he'll be gled
That comin hame's the anely answer.

His makar's een look richt up there
At the dowie lift o Hungary:
He'll greet and tremmle never mair.   .

The Magyar sun shines on its weans.
At hame, he'll dream aboot the Med:
At hame, the craws'll pick his banes.

Nice/Nizza, 1907.

2006

BIRTHPLACE

From the Hungarian of Endre Ady

There's Sanct Benedick's hill - dae ye no see it?
An unco place, thon brae: and I've heard tell
There wis a cloister whiles, upby. They say
That through the haar - the nicht or Benedick's day -
A touer leams white, wi dunnlin o its bell.

And this is Ér, oor burn,
Thon *noble ditch* o Kraszna, sae they cried it.
Nou it's sair dried-up, aa cracked.
Leddy: wad ye care for't gin I plucked
Some twa-three withert flouers that lig inside it?

Here is Kotó, yince a village,
That wis yirdit, cowpit bi the Turks lang syne.
Juist legends and the odd traces nou.
If you please, leddy: *efter you*,
Inti oor village: here's the path we jyne.

This is the village, my clachan,
I wis born here and I come back.
It's cried *All Saints*, but why, ye'd never guess,
For it's acquent wi nocht but wickitness
That grups yer thrapple, and fair damns ye black.

And here's my verra sel,
The auld firebrand's nou a heap o stour.
My weird whistles abüne us twa:
Flee frae me, curse me, hate me an-aa,
Else haud me blythely in *high honour* ...

2006

It was the poet Győző Ferencz who introduced me – in the unlikely setting of a Kirkcaldy café – to the paintings of Tivadar Csontváry Kosztka (1853-1919) and I was immediately hooked. His work can be related to Symbolism and to naïve art (l'art brut) but only up to a point – he's unique.

His very name is not without interest. 'Csont' in Hungarian means 'bone'.

THE PAINTER TIVADAR CSONTVÁRY

for Győző Ferencz

The great ridges of the Tatra
Rising rough and filling with their light
The valley of the Tarpatak.

An October afternoon,
And the pharmacist's assistant
Reached for his charcoal:
He was both drawn and drawing.

His boss tapped him on the shoulder,
Not rebuking.
'You are a natural artist.'

Once he picked up from the stones
A three-cornered seed:
In his soul it would grow
To the solitary cedar.

The cedar spread its sinuous branches
(One with the neck and head of a strange bird)
Across an Asian steppe.

An outcrop turreted in the mist
Might be the dungeon of a voivode:
Alone the cedar asserted peace.

Both messiah and pilgrim,
He headed south and east
Like Bartók in the Arab lands
Augmenting his own native tones.

'Eagle and poet
May look into the sun:
But owls and the night stars
Hate what they fear.'

He sat in a neuk
Of the artists' coffee-house
They called the *Japan*:
No-one spoke to him
Except in mockery.

But in the gallery
On Buda Castle Hill,
A woman at the mezzanine
Is sitting on a bench
For what seems an hour
Gazing at nothing else
But Csontváry's *Ruins*
Of the Theatre at Taormina.

2004

UKRAINE

BONNY KATE

The tragic tale of Katerina, as related by the national poet Shevchenko (1814-61), is a Ukrainian ballad which seemed to me to have potential as a Scottish one, so here goes.

BONNY KATE

From the Ukrainian of Taras Shevchenko

Katie welcomes guests
    Ti her domain:
There's three Cossack lawds
    Her favour wad gain.

The first wis Simon Barefuit,
    The saicond, Scuddie Jock;
The third wis Seán, the weedow's son,
    A braw-like kinna stock.

'We've stravaiged throu Poland,
    Forby Ukraine;
But bonnier queans nor Katie here,
    Be shair we met wi nane.'

The first chiel said: 'Gin I wis rich,
    Bi-Gode, I tell ye, sir,
I'd gie up ilka lest bawbee
    Fir wan wee oor wi her.'

The saicond said: 'Gin I wis strang,
    I'd tell ye, boys, my fate –
Frae he-man I'd turn wallydrag,
    Fir wan wee oor wi Kate.'

The third loun says: 'Ye're haverin, min:
    Listen ti me – I'm sassy –
There's bugger-aa I wadna dae
    Ti lie doun wi this lassie.'

Katie taks tent: she speaks
    Ti gallánt number three:
'My ainly brither's in the jyle,
    And I wish he wis free!

'Dounby in Crimea,
    They bunged him inside:
Wha brings him ti me,
    I'll become that man's bride!'

Sae aa three set aff,
    Each upon his cuddy.
'Lads! Lat's dae white'er it taks
    Ti free her brither-body.'

The first boy, he drouned
    Whan the river lowped the dyke;
The saicond fell amang his faes,
    Impaled upon a spike.

The third, he hauds forrit,
    The braw-like weedow's son:
Lowses the leddy's brither –
    Be shair, thon bride he's won!

The door's fair creakin
    Up the big-hoose, at the crack
O dawn.
            'Kate! Oot o yer lazy-bed,
    Yer brither dear's come back.'

Kate's greetin, Kate's smilin:
    'I tellt ye a lee:
Fir thon's no my brither,
    But my jo, come back ti me.'

'Ye bluidy hüre!' cries big braw Seán.
  'Ye led me on, and hou!'
He swacks her heid richt aff her corp,
  And she's no bonny nou.

'Come, brither dear,' cries big braw Seán.
  'Lat's quit this hoose o sin.'
Thir horsemen skelp athort the steppe,
  The winds ower-raxin.

Daurk-broued Kate
  In the park wis beeried:
And on the steppe twa Cossacks swore
  Bluid-britherheid.

2012

RUSSIA

VARIATION RUSSE
THE PERMITTED AND THE POSSIBLE
CHEKHOVIANA

Now for some short poems from a large country, with reference to three of its greatest writers. We start with a compression of Dostoyevsky with the tale of Lizzie Borden, the young Massachusetts girl who seriously fell out with her parents, and became the subject of a skipping-rhyme echoed here. Dostoyevsky's own comic gifts are not always recognised: his work is all-encompassing, so even Crime and Punishment *is not without its buffooneries, albeit of the darker sort. 'If you want to see into a man and to understand his soul', he wrote in his late novel* A Raw Youth, *'don't concentrate your attention on the way he talks or is silent, or his tears, or the emotion he displays over lofty ideas. You'll see through him better when he laughs.'*

I have an inkling that Dostoyevsky would have approved of this variation on another popular rhyme:

> If only the just were funny,
>   If only the funny were just,
> We'd have to give up: anger, pride and gluttony,
>   Envy, sloth, avarice, and lust.

VARIATION RUSSE SUR UN THÈME FOLKLORIQUE AMÉRICAIN

Roddy Raskolnikov with an axe
Hit the pawnbroker forty whacks.
When she saw what he had done
He hit her stepsister forty-one.

2008

A quarter of a century ago, Philip Roth made a remark that has passed into common (or perhaps more accurately, uncommon) parlance; like all such remarks that become part of oral tradition, its wording has metamorphosed somewhat. The gist of it, though, is that in the West, everything is permitted but nothing matters, whereas in the East nothing is permitted but everything matters. That seemed to relate very strongly to Isaiah Berlin's reminiscence of Russian public transport, where you could hear young girls avidly discussing the works of the nineteenth-century novelist Turgenev. Like other Russian expatriates, Turgenev lived for a while in Baden-Baden, the spa town in south-western Germany.

THE PERMITTED AND THE POSSIBLE

On buses, way back,
Young girl Muscovites
Of Turgenev's *Rudin*
Warmly debating –

Now, under his plaque,
The footballers' wives
In Baden-Baden
Shop for bling.

2009

The following poem was written as a tribute to Angus Calder (1942-2008), the Scottish poet, historian, critic, cultural / political activist and Russophile. Some years before his death, I had heard that he was looking forward to re-reading Chekhov's short stories, from which a number of motifs appear in the poem. Angus's Russia Discovered *(1976), a long out-of-print account of Pushkin, Gogol, Dostoyevsky, Tolstoy, Chekhov et al, needs to be reissued and itself rediscovered.*

CHEKHOVIANA

By the estuary of abandoned islands
Stand the lonely family man and the lady with dog,
The waves enfolding before and after their days:

Below the castle crag
At the gate of the pleasure garden, a woman weeps
For those she had loved, who sickened in the mists:
She clasps desperately the hand of her adopted child.

Yakov the widower regrets unspoken tenderness,
Praises the lissom birch-tree, yields up his fiddle.
Another weaves a cell round himself, or gorges his
                                gooseberry-patch.

'Let a man with a hammer constantly bash on
                                the doors
Of the prosperous. Why wait at the edge of a ditch,
While it slowly filths up, when I can jump or
                                bridge it?'

At the wayside inn, with his small peevish daughter,
A lyrical migrant worker gives his life-story
To a beautiful stranger. History cranks and screeches
                                about them,

As folk lose one faith and stumble into another.

2008

EPILOGUE

THE TINT THREID

On that 1989 Demarco 'expedition' – mentioned earlier – to Poland, I took with me an anthology of Polish women poets, Ariadne's Thread *(Forest Books, 1988). I was not so much surprised as impressed that, in Poland at that time, so many art works, theatres and theatre pieces had the Polish word 'labirynt' in their title, or otherwise deployed the image of the labyrinth, which instantly suggests one of the oldest European myths.*

Moreover, so many Polish theatre spaces, occupying attics or cellars, seemed themselves to be labyrinthine. In many ways, the widening chinks in the Iron Curtain revealed an Alice-through-the-looking-glass world, where assumed meanings and certainties would slip into their opposites. This was not only a Polish phenomenon, but an east / central European one – hadn't the Scottish poet Edwin Muir represented Prague as a labyrinth? You never knew what would be round the corner ...

THE TINT THREID/ THE LOST THREAD

*How if there were no centre at all, but just one
alley after another, and the whole world a labyrinth
without end or issue?*

ROBERT LOUIS STEVENSON

The Seeker

Frae lair ti lair, I weave my wey in vain;
A waa looms up, and baurs the likeliest wynd;
A licht glimmers and growes, then aa's in mirk,
And whaur I stertit oot, I canna mynd.
Suddent I come upon a keekin-gless,
That shaws my librarie, whaur I can tell
Its raws, its buiks, by hert; but whit reflects
Lauchs soorly at my warld, and at mysel.

The Bairn Unborn

Mither, tak my haund. Come, dinna leave my side:
I am shair-fuitit and I winna faa.
My senses gain in clearness. Warm and wide
Is the luve that melts this limbo fir us twa.

The Seeker

Hou suid I hear o luve? Oor anerlie heat
Brust frae the terrible wrack o toun, o gate,
O hoose, o fowk: the lowe heezed up frae the deep,
And the least o bairns wis smuirit in the hate.
Gin thon's a voice that cries me at my side,

I'm sair owerhailit fir ti mak it oot:
I'm the stravaiger wha aye gangs her lane,
I'm the believer maist acquent wi doobt.

The Bairn Unborn

Mither, you greet; that gars me greet alsweill,
But I wad lauch, fir this my life is new;
My baum wad your maist gantin stab-wounds heal;
My braith wad clear the reek, that thrapples you.

The Seeker

That voice bydes on … I hear it doun the years,
It aichoes throu the cellars o oor pain;
Ower mony ghaists, ti stalk us throu oor tears,
Ower mony ghaists, the warld's, and oor ain.
O I am an earn that wad beat her wings ti the lift,
But I am hauden-doun by huidiecraws;
Gin they cuid wile me aince inside their net,
They'd teir my corp ti pieces wi their claws.

The Bairn Unborn

Mither, dinna be feart. I am nae ghaist,
Nor wane wi caundles, wither wi the flouers.

The Seeker

Your presence rests me, maks me even-paced,
And the hunneryears that pass, are anerlie oors …

The Bairn

Oot o this mirk, you wove a wey fir me;

You dwyne awa as I tak up the threid;
Tho it be fankled, I sall lowse it free,
Tho it be riven, my skeil sall mak remeid.
You bid me link at this richt furthily,
O mither, newly welcomed wi the deid:
Fir thaim, fir you, fir aa wha follow me,
I'll twyne thir sacrit straunds o white and reid.

1989

GLOSSARY

A

aa all
aabody everybody
ablow below, beneath
aboot about
abüne above
acquent acquainted
aff off
afore before
Afrikie Africa
aften often
aftentimes often
aheid ahead
ahent behind
aichoes echoes
ain own
airches arches
airms arms
airts districts, areas,
    directions
aise-midden ash-heap
aither either
alsweill also, as well
amang among
an-aa also, as well
    (and all)
ane one
anely only

anerlie only
aneth beneath
apairt apart
aroond around
athort across
atween between
auld old
auncient ancient
awa away
awin own
aye still, always
ayont beyond

B

bade lived, dwelt
bairns children
baith both
banes bones
banket banquet
Barefuit Barefoot
baum balm
baund band
baurs bars
Bavairie Bavaria
bawbee coin of least
    value
beeried buried
befoir before
ben mountain
bi by
bield(s) shelter(s)
biggit built
big-hoose big house,
    manor

bit little
bi-Gode by God
birl(ed) whirl(ed), dance(d), turn(ed around
blaws blows
blackened blackened
blenk glance
blenking expression
blethered talked idly
bluid blood
bluid-britherheid blood-brotherhood
bluid-reid blood-red
bluidy bloody
blythely happily
blytheness happiness
brae-face hillside
brainches branches
braisantlie boldly
braith breath
braw beautiful, handsome, impressive
braw-like beautiful, impressive, drop-dead gorgeous
breist breast
brennin burning
bricht bright
brither brother
brocht brought
brou brow, summit
brust(s) burst(s)
bugger-aa bugger-all

buik(s) book(s)
buirdliest most impressive, magnificent
buiths shops (booths)
burds birds
burn stream, small river, creek, beck
byde(s) stay(s), remain(s),
bydin waiting, delaying, remaining; can also mean: dwelling, resident

C

caa call
cairry carry
cam came
canna cannot
cauldrife cold, cold-causing
caundles candles
chaunce chance
cheenge change
chiel person, fellow
chowk choke
chynged changed
clachan village
clachan-fuit village-end, foot of village
clanked imprisoned, confined
cleevin cleft

cleikit clutched, caught
cobwabs cobwebs
con squirrel
conjoinit conjoined
conquessed conquered
coorse course
corp body, corpse
courin cowering
cowp heap (of ruins), sometimes rubbish heap, pile of discarded stuff
cowpit ruined, destroyed
craigs rocks
craws crows
cried called
crummles crumbles
crummlin crumbling
cryne(s) recoil(s), shrink(s), withdraw(s)
cuddy horse
cuid could
cuik cook

D

dae do
daffin playful, bantering in a loving manner
daid dead
daith death
daithlie deathly
daunce dance
dauncin dancing
dauner dander, stroll
daurk dark
daurk-broued dark-browed
daurna dares not
dearlie dearly
deaved annoyed, pestered, bored
dee die
deid-bell passing-bell, death-bell, death-knell
depairt depart
dern hidden
dert(s) dart(s) [verb and noun]
ding doun pull down, destroy
dirl(in) vibrat(e)(ing), reverberate(ing)
dochter daughter
doolie gloomy
doun down
dounby down there
dowie gloomy
dowp backside, posterior, arse
drap drop
dreich dreary
drouned drowned
drounin drowning
drouth thirst
drow drizzle
drumlie troubled,

gloomy, cloudy
dubs puddles
dug dog
dule sadness, stress,
trouble
dun fortress
düne done
dunner clatter,
reverberation
dunnlin tolling,
reverberating
dwyne dwindle
dyke wall

E

earn eagle
een eyes
eenou even now
efter after
efterkin descendants
eidently diligently
eldritch weird, uncanny
emerant emerald
ene eyes
eneuch enough
engowfed engulfed
ettled tried, attempted
ever-twynin ever-
twisting and
turning

F

faa fall
faes foes
faither father
fankled tangled
fash trouble
faur far
feart afraid
fechtin fighting
feenished finished
feres comrades
ferlie wonder, marvel
ferms farms
fest fast
fir for
flair floor
flichterin fluttering,
palpitating
flouers flowers
foontains fountains
forby moreoever,
besides
fore-end beginning
forefolk ancestors
forefowk ancestors
(fore-folk)
forehand first, foremost
forrit forward
fortrace fortress
fou full
foustie fusty, mouldy
fowk folk
frae from
fremmit strange(ly),
unfamiliar(ly),

foreign, alien
friens friends
fu full
fufft blew gently, wafted
furth forth
furthily boldly,
    impulsively
fyke fuss

G

gaed went
gairden garden
gang go
gantin gaping
gar cause, make happen
ghaists ghosts
gie give
gien gave
gie ower give up,
    renounce
gin if
glaikit foolish, daft,
    besotted
glaur mud
gled glad
gleg quick, ready, off
    the mark
glintit glinted
glisked glanced
glisterin glistening,
    glittering
gloamin twilight, dusk
gowdblinterin gold-
    glimmering

grat wept
greet weep
gresslaund grassland,
    pasture
grippy tight-fisted, mean
growes grows
growthie fertile
growthily abundantly
gruggilt disfigured
grups grips
guaird guard
guid good
gurgin surging

H

haar thick mist, fog, on
    the east coast of
    Scotland
hae have
hairst autumn, fall
    (harvest)
hairt heart
hale whole
halflin youth,
    adolescent,
    immature young
    man
hame home
hamelaund homeland
hark at listen to
harns brains
haud hold
hauden-doun oppressed,
    tyrannised (held

down)

hauds forrit keeps on, continues (holds forward)

haund(s) hand(s)

haverin talking nonsense

heezed rose, raised

heich high

heich-heidit arrogant, full of oneself (high-headed)

heid head

heid-bummer boss, posh guy at the top, king of the midden

hert heart

himsel himself

hing hang

hinner-end hinder-end, last phase

hit's it's

hoose house

hotterin seething

hou how

howff pub (can also mean graveyard, burial ground)

howp hope

huidiecraws sinister persons in charge and dispensing 'justice', time-servers, creepy control freaks

(hooded crows)

hunneryears centuries (hundred years)

hüre whore

I

i in

inby within

inti into

ilka each

ill-thriven not thriving, undeveloped, under-nourished

ither(s) other(s)

itsel itself

J

jalouse imagine

jiggin dancing generally (i.e. not necessarily dancing a jig)

jing-bang (the whole) lot of it, caboodle

jo sweetheart, lover

juist just

jyle jail

jyled jailed

jylers jailors

jyne join

K

keekin-gless mirror

100

(looking-glass)
ken know
kent knew, known
kest(s) casts
kinna kind of
kinrik kingdom
kintra country
kirkyaird churchyard,
burial ground

L

lair lair, grave, mire
lane alone (**my lane** by
myself, alone)
lang long
lang-cowpit long-
ruined, long-
demolished
lang-deid long-dead
lang syne long ago
larick larch
lat let
lat's let us (let's)
lauch laugh
laucht laughed
laund land
lave remainder
lawdie lad (laddie), boy,
fellow
lazar-houss leper-house
leam gleam of light
leared learned
leddies ladies
lee lie

leevin living
leid language
leman lover
lest last
leuk(it) look(ed)
licht light
lift sky
lig lie
liltit lilted, sang
link at act speedily and
vigorously
linn river, stream
loan paddock
loun fellow, boy
lowe flame, glow
lowped jumped, leaped
lowses frees, releases
lowsin-time knocking-
off time, end of
work shift
lugs ears
luvers lovers
luves loves
lythe calm

M

macklike suitable,
appropriate
mair more
mairch border
mairrit on married to
maist most
maister(s) master(s)
mak make

101

makar poet (maker)
mane moan
manheid manhood
maun must
mavie mavis, song
    thrush
Med Mediterranean
mell mingle
melled mixed, blended
min man
mirk darkness
mishanter misfortune,
    disaster
mistak mistake
mitherlaund motherland
modren modern
mony many
mony-thoosand many-
    thousand(s)
morn, the the next day /
    morning, tomorrow
mou mouth
muckle big
muild mould, cast
muivement movement
muives moves
murn mourn
murtherin murdering
mynd remember, mind
mysel myself

N

nae no, not
naebody nobody

nairra narrow
nane none, nobody
neath beneath
neuk corner, nook
nevermair nevermore
nicht night
no not
nocht not, nothing
nor than
nou now

O

o of
objeck object
ony any
oor (1) our (2) hour
oot out
or before
ower too, over
owerhailit oppressed,
    overcome
ower-raxin over-
    reaching, coming
    upon, overtaking,
    catching up with

P

pad path
pairt part
pairty party
park field
peeriest smallest
peety pity

pentins paintings
pey pay
peyed paid
peyson poison
pit put
plantit planted
ply distress, plight
port (city / town) gate
prieve prove
prieven proven
prood proud
puir poor
puirtith poverty
purpie purple

Q

quait quiet
queans girls, young
  women

R

raible rabble
rair(ed) roar(ed)
raither rather
raws rows
reamin foaming,
  frothing
recks na doesn't care
  (cares not)
reek smoke
reid red
remeid remedy
retour return

richt right
rickle heap, pile
rugged dragged
ruit root

S

sacrit sacred
sae so
saicond second
saicont second
saicret sacred
sair sore(ly)
sall shall
sang(s) song(s)
saucht peace (of mind),
  serenity
scho she
schuil school
sclaves slaves
Scuddie Bare, Naked
seg sedge
seilfu soulful
seiven seven
sel self
shair-fuitit sure-footed
shairly surely
shaws shows
shoogle quaking,
  shaking
sib like, similar to, akin
sic such
siccar sure, secure,
  reliable
siccarlie surely, certainly

sicht sight
siclike suchlike
simmer summer
sin since
skaith trouble, hurt
skeil skill
skelp gallop
skinkles glistens
skreek screech, scream
skufft struck off, swept away
slauchter slaughter
slaw slow
slockened quenched
smitch(es) speck(s), little bit(s), trace(s)
smuirit smothered
snaw-flaucht snow-flake
sneck lock, shut
sodger soldier
sonsie buxom, comely
sooch gentle wind, breeze
sook suck
soorly sourly
soun sound
spae foretell
speir ask
speirins questions
spreid spread
stane(s) stone(s)
starns stars
staun(s) stand(s)
stecht stuffed full
steidit founded, placed

steir stir
stertit started
stock fellow, guy
stour dust
strachts streets
straiks strokes
stramash uproar, tumult
strang strong
straunds strands
stravaiged wandered, travelled
stravaiger wanderer
stuid stood
suddent suddenly
suid should
süne soon
süner sooner
swacks strikes
sweit sweat
sweyin swaying
syne since, since then, ago, previously

T

tae too, also
taen taken
taks tent takes note, ponders
tellt told
tentless heedless
tenty (o) attentive / alert (to), aware (of)
thaim them
the-day today

104

thegither together
theirsels themselves
thir those
thocht thought
thon that
thousan thousand
thrapple throat
thrapples throttles
threid thread
threipin asserting insistently, harping on
thristin thrusting
throu through
ti to
tichtened tightened
timorsome timorous
tint lost
touer tower
touerin towering
toun town
trauchle struggle
tremmle tremble
tuik took
tumeness emptiness
twa two
tweests twists
twinty twenty
twyne twine

U

umwhile former
uncheenged unchanged
unco uncanny

unner under
untentit neglected, ignored
upby up there
uptaen taken up, interested, preoccupied

V

vainishes vanishes
vennel narrow lane between buildings
verra very
virr energy, vigour, force

W

waas walls
wabbit tired, exhausted
wabsters weavers
wad would
wadna would not
wae woe
wale majority
wallydrag weak, puny, insignificant creature, runt
wan one
wark work
warld world
warsle struggle
wasters people who waste other people's time and

who are themselves
a waste of space,
idlers

weedow widow

weans children

weill well

weir war

weird fate

weirdit fateful, fated

wey way

wha who

whan when

whase whose

whaur where

wheegees whims,
gewgaws,
trivialities

whiles at one time,
formerly

whit what

white'er it taks whatever
it takes

whyles at times

wickitness wickedness

winna will not

wis was

wisna was not

withert withered

wowf wolf

wrack wreck (noun
and verb),
destruction,
destroy

wrocht made, wrought,
built

wuids woods

wyce wise

wynd narrow lane or
street

Y

yett gate

yin one

yince once

yirdit buried

yit yet

ACKNOWLEDGMENTS

My thanks to the editors and publishers of the following, in which versions of these poems first appeared: *Asheville Poetry Review, Behind the Lines, Berlioz Society Bulletin, Brindin Press website, Cencrastus, Chapman, Epona, Fife Lines* (Swiss issue), *Four Fife Poets, For Angus, Fras, Fringe Of Gold, Handfast, Isolde's Luve-Daith, Lallans, Lines Review, Markings, The New Makars, Peacocks and Squirrels, Poetry Salzburg Review, Radical Scotland, Sax Sonnets in Scots, Scots Glasnost, Scottish PEN Members' Blog, Scrievins, Seguendo la traccia, Tak 5 / Tak 50, Twa Leids / Da Chànain, West Coast Magazine.*

I am grateful to Mario Relich for providing an introduction to the collection, and to Gonzalo Mazzei for once again making possible a book-length harvesting of my work from a quarter of a century and more.

There are a number of translations in the present collection; I am indebted to the following for their expertise in the source languages: Eberhard Bort, Dominique Delmaire, Heidelinde Prüger, Emília Szaffner, Zsuzsanna Varga, James Wilkie.

Further thanks, for advice and encouragement here and there, are due to Margaret Bennett, Kenny Munro, Tessa Ransford and James Robertson.

The author would like to record his appreciation of Arkady Pugachevsky's generosity in allowing us to use his engraving on the cover.

BIBLIOGRAPHICAL NOTES

PROLOGUE: SCOTLAND
The Retour o Troilus

First published in the magazine *Cencrastus*, issue no.
24 (Autumn 1986), and reprinted in *Four Fife Poets*
(anthology; Aberdeen UP, 1988), *The New Makars*
(anthology; The Mercat Press, 1991), *Twa Leids /
Dà Chànan* (bilingual anthology [Scots and Gaelic];
Scotsoun, 1994), *Peacocks and Squirrels* (solo collection;
Akros, 2007). I read the poem for a recording made by
the late Dr George Philp for a Scotsoun audiocassette,
which was accompanied by the aforementioned
Twa Leids anthology; a 2002 CD, *Tak 5 / Tak 50*, also
recorded and compiled by Dr Philp for Scotsoun,
includes a reissue of my performance of the poem. A
Gaelic translation of the poem, by Uilleam Nèill (the
late William Neill), appeared in *Gairm*, aireamh 142
(an-t-Earrach 1988), and in *Twa Leids* (with the Gaelic
version read by Coinneach Dòmhnallach). An Italian
translation, by Andrea Fabbri, appeared in *Seguendo
la traccia* (bilingual anthology [Scots and Italian];
Mobydick, 1997).

BELGIUM
European Capital

Previously published in the anthology *Behind the Lines*
(Third Eye Centre, 1989), with an illustration by Willie
Rodger.

FRANCE
Berlioz at Meylan
Previously published in the magazine *Chapman*, no. 80 (1995), and discussed in Michael Wright, 'Berlioz in Poetry', *The Berlioz Society Bulletin*, no. 154 (Winter 1995).
Edgar Poe
Previously published in the magazine *Fras*, no. 17 (2012). The original poem appeared in Rollinat's collection *Les névroses* (Charpentier, Paris, 1883).

SPAIN
El Greco Variations
Previously published as part of a narrative poem, 'The Temptation of Michael Scot', in my pamphlet collection *Scottish Faust* (Kettillonia, 2004).

ITALY
Pompeii
Previously published in *Lines Review*, no. 96 (March 1986), *Four Fife Poets* (Aberdeen UP, 1988), and *Lines Review*, 40th Anniversary Celebration issue: Poems through the Years 1952-1992, no. 120 (March 1992). A Gaelic translation by Uilleam Nèill (William Neill) appeared in *Gairm*, aireamh 145 (an Geamhradh 1988-89). My reading of the poem can be heard on the 2002 Scotsoun CD *Tak 5 / Tak 50*.
Paolo to Francesca
Previously published in *Scrievins: the Magazine for Fife Writing*, double issue 4/5 (Summer / Autumn 1987).
Catullus LXI
Prevously published in *Handfast: Scottish Poems for Weddings and Affirmations* (Scottish Poetry Library / Polygon, 2004).

La madre dei laghi
Previously published in *Lines Review*, no. 143 (December 1997), and in my pamphlet collection *Isolde's Luve-Daith* (Akros, 1998).

GERMANY
Speirins
Previously published in *Radical Scotland* (December / January 1989). The original poem, 'Fragen eines lesenden Arbeiters', was composed by Brecht in exile and first appeared in the Moscow-based magazine *Das Wort* in 1936.
Laachersee Elegy
Previously published in the magazine *Markings*, Special 10th Anniversary double issue, nos. 20 and 21 (2004).
Schellbronn
Previously published in my pamphlet *Sax Sonnets in Scots* (Scrievins, 1987), and in *Four Fife Poets* (Aberdeen UP, 1988). I recorded the poem for the *Tak 5 / Tak 50 CD* (Scotsoun, 2002).

SWITZERLAND
The Terrace at Basel
Previously published in the *Poetry Salzburg Review*, no. 4 (Spring 2003).
Frae A Vocatioun o Rivers
Previously published in *Lallans*, nummer 59 (Hairst 2001), which carried a special feature of Swiss poetry translated into Scots. Maurice Chappaz's original poem, *Vocation des fleuves*, was published by La Joie de Lire of Geneva in 1998.
An Antiquarian Print
Previously published in *Fife Lines*, Poetry from Switzerland issue, no. 6 (Autumn 2002). Duchosal's original poem, 'Sur une ancienne estampe', appeared

in his collection *Le livre de Thulé* (Editions Eggimann, Geneva, 1891).

AUSTRIA
Music at Kufstein
Previously published in *Scots Glasnost*, no. 2 (1989).
Iceberg
Previously published, together with the original poem, 'Eisberg', at The Brindin Press online anthology of translations, at http://www.brindin.com/; click on Poems-German.

POLAND
Candles
Previously published in *West Coast Magazine*, issue 8 (1991); Gaelic translation by Uilleam Nèill in *Gairm*, aireamh 189 (an Geamhradh 1999-2000); Hungarian translation by Győző Ferencz in *Nagyvilág*, 9-10 (1966), reprinted in the anthology *Skót bárdok, magyar költők* (Ráció Kiadó, Budapest, 2007).

HUNGARY
Himnusz
Previosuly published in the online journal *Epona*, 1 (2007) at http://www.bdf.hu/btk/flli/anglisztika/epona-journal. The original poem, which became the words of the Hungarian national anthem, was composed by Kölcsey in 1823.
Red Hedgehog
Previously published in the *Asheville Poetry Review*, vol. 5, no. 1 (1998), as part of a 'Budapest Diary' of my period as a visiting lecturer in the spring of 1996.
Hame Thochts, Frae the Med
Birthplace
Both previously published in *Epona*, 1 (2007): see

above, *Himnusz*. Ady's original poems appeared in the collections *Vér és arany [Blood and Gold]* (1907; 'Hame Thochts' as 'Hazavágyás Napfény-országból') and *Szeretném ha szeretnének [I Would Love to be Loved]* (1909; 'Birthplace' as 'Séta bölcső-helyem körül').
The Painter Tivadar Csontváry
Previously published in *Fras*, 11 (2009).

UKRAINE
Bonny Kate
Not previously published, but first performed at the 'Kávéház at Curlers' event, Glasgow, 5 December 2012, organised by Dr Zsuzsanna Varga of Glasgow University. Shevchenko's original ballad ('U tieï Katerini …') dates from 1848.

RUSSIA
Variation russe …
This squib appears here for the first time.
The Permitted and the Possible
Not previously published.
Chekhoviana
Previously published in *For Angus: Poems, Prose, Sketches and Music, May-July 2008* (Los Poetry Press, Cambridge, 2009).

EPILOGUE
The Tint Threid
This appears here for the first time.

ABOUT THE AUTHOR

TOM HUBBARD was born in 1950 and educated at Aberdeen and Strathclyde Universities. His books include the 'cosmopolitan' novel *Marie B.* (2008), which was longlisted for a Saltire award, and the poetry collection *The Chagall Winnocks* (2011). He is currently completing a second novel, a black farce set in his native Fife and drawing on folklore. He writes in English and Scots, mainly on international themes.

He was the first librarian of the Scottish Poetry Library and went on to become an itinerant academic. In 2011-12 he was, successively, Lynn Wood Neag Distinguished Visiting Professor at the University of Connecticut, Professeur invité at the Stendhal University, Grenoble, and a Writer-in-residence at the Château Lavigny in Vaud, Switzerland.

On Seeking Mr Hyde:
'a slim volume of considerable depth and insight'. (Hazel Hynd in the *Scottish Literary Journal*: the Year's Work).

On The Integrative Vision:
'He mentions in his introduction the concept he had, in the old days of the Scottish Poetry Library, of poetry as "a base-camp, a starting-point rather than a destination" and he refers to an Eskimo word meaning both to make poetry and to breathe [...] [He] has been welcomed over the past 20 years as a visiting professor spreading the integrative vision on the arts and literature across Europe, America and Ireland. Now he is back in the Kingdom of Fife concentrating on a second novel and

further poems and translations.' (Tessa Ransford in the *Scottish Review*, 20 December 2012).

On Tak 5 / Tak 50:
'his poems gie ye yon oorie metaphysical trummle doun the backbane' (Ann Matheson in *Lallans*).

On Scottish Faust:
'There's depth here' (Robert R. Calder in *Lallans*).

On Marie B.:
'I loved this book, not least because of all that it did not say. The spaces and silences are as eloquent as the writing. But of course that is exactly as it should be, given that this is a book by a poet about what it means to be an artist' (Catherine Czerkawska in the *Edinburgh Review*).

On The Chagall Winnocks:
'At stake is not just parity of poetic esteem for Scots but the status of the spoken and written word in general.' (Michael Kerrigan in the *Scotsman*, with a four-star rating for the book).

'The Chagall at wrocht the winnocks in the sang at gies the haill buik its teitle wes a Jewish limner at wes born in Belarus, bade whiles in Russia, whiles in France an whiles in America, shapit the winnocks for a kirk in Germany, an nou inspeirit a braw sang frae a Scottish makar. Is thon no cosmopolitanism? Here we hae as bonnie a pruif as ye coud wiss tae finn o hou the Scottish speirit is maist national whan maist international. Scottish cultuir in its best times tuik whit it hed need o frae ither airts, an paid back the debt wi interest. Scotland mairches shouther tae shouther wi fowerteen ither kintras in Tam Hubbard's winnersome ingetherin.' (J. Derrick McClure in *Lallans*).

20598506R00068

Made in the USA
Charleston, SC
19 July 2013